welcome to the campfire

Akshay Chougaonkar

Published by Perceiving Things
Copyright © Akshay Chougaonkar 2021

ISBN 978-0-6450711-0-8

Front cover and book design by nuejist
Photo by meiandc

First published 2021
Perceiving Things
Sydney, Australia

www.perceivingthings.com

My sincerest gratitude to nuejist, without whose help the book wouldn't look as beautiful as it does. Thank you for designing the book cover and organizing the interior layout design.

Thank You To The Artists Who Contributed...

Autumn Memoir I - Sharvari

i am second year mbbs student. in my free time i love reading books and artsy stuff.

Autumn Memoir II - Tanvi

Autumn Memoir III - Chinmay

i am a computer science undergrad at birla institute of technology, mesra. i belong to the cult that turns caffeine into code, yup, i'm a programmer. i can be usually found in front of my laptop, fumbling with my keyboard and vibing to a linkin park or eminem song. i enjoy reading in my spare time or watching web series or anime, but for me, nothing beats the thrill of a coding contest, with the timer running and the standings changing drastically every 15 mins or so, and that green tick that appears after i solve a problem correctly. aah, i guess i went too far, that's about it from me then.

The Farm - Achyut

i am a ph.d. in management, an academic and researcher with award-winning as well as best-selling case studies in management. i was a blogger who later took to writing on quora where i was also awarded top writer 2018. i enjoy doing creative things like drawing portraits, writing, poetry, blogging, playing the piano, cricket, sports and games, taekwondo, solving rubik's cube, am a self taught skater, bo staff twirler and spiritual seeker.

Saturn's Joy - Aishwarya

Like The Paper Boat - Amruta

Dear reader,

Let us delight in life's tiny pleasures abundant,
But seldom felt.

contents

...

Welcome to the campfire...

Prologue:

Dusk

13

Gather around, fellow Wanderers, around this campfire here.
The firewood has now embraced the fire
And shall soon generate warmth for us all to share.

Soon the flame shall thrive, with a music of its own
And wee embers, like countless glow worms, in suspension
Shall dance to breezes that, hither, have thus far blown.

When the dusk bids a farewell, amid musings myriad, together
In our quilt of warmth we shall script around this campfire,
A wintry night, beside this gleaming ocean sapphire.

Songs we shall sing, of people and of places
And if we let our gazes adrift, some of these faces and places
Can be spotted hither, around us under a canopy of stars.

As this campfire ages, like this night still in bloom,
May a homage be paid to dear autumn,
Now bygone, blanketed in chills and by time consumed.

Gathered wanderers, lost souls, dreamers and lovers!
Feel the solace of comforting warmth and meek kisses
Of winter's chills, like intimacy, amid sorrows and bliss.

Slumber enthralled horizon shall soon awaken, signaling dawn
Mellowing the campfire—a plea for us to discern (in a pious tone)
Known to man, yet much unnoticed joys around and transcendent
fancies.

At dawn, when the campfire has grown old and wise—
Scintillating and smouldering—and now mere embers,
Moments of tranquil contemplations doth our beauteous
bower deserves; for it was here, amid deep seclusion,
Together, we rejoiced in raptures of yore,
Half extinguished intimacies and unremembered pleasures.

Nightfall

shadows on the ceiling

Late at night
When sleep sets in
And the mind starts to
Fade away, it
Amuses itself,
Perplexed at
Frolicking shadows
On the ceiling.

From sources
Unbeknownst,
Illuminating
Faintly,
The ceiling—
The canvas—
Your life
In the night,
Those dim lights
Entice the shadows
Up on the ceiling—
The stage—
And their faces,
Silhouettes
Persistent to
Remain clad
In a mystery.

In moments like these
When mind pays no heed
To this light so wee,
Perceiving shadows of trees
As faces that deceive,
Sleep—
Embrace this darkness;
It will pacify
Your mind
Lost amid
Shadows on the ceiling.

Seldom do I realise,
Wandering whispers of the night
Like ghouls waltzing passionately
Under the glinting starry lights.

Caressing my ears,
Delusional fears
Their joyous plea,
Under the moon's canopy.

Serene peace lurks
Screaming epic fables.
Streams of euphoric chills
Savour my tormenting perils.

My senses surrender
To this silence abound,
Whilst I lay mesmerised
Amidst these whispers; nirvana bound.

Seldom do I realise,
Wandering whispers of the night.

set the moon free

Have you ever seen the moon
Through the trees, sieving in
Its light on wintry nights?
Oh! Someone has cast these nets
To catch the moon.

In these woods, with chilly winds
And countless stars around,
The moon is clad not in fog nor clouds,
Yet, she has no complaints
About her being caught.

She resists not to flailing trees
Clutching her so tight oft-times,
Nay she drowns in their ripe medley
While I stand beneath these trees
Wishing I could set her free.

ravens

Menacing,
The night persists
Haunting cities
Patrolled by these chilly winds
And ravens alike.

Lapping their wings,
The ravens challenge the winds,
Perching on rooftops
And gargoyles.
Their eyes,
A purposeful black void,
Holding Odin's ever-seeking light
For the courageous
And the mighty,
Delivering prophecies.

An ominous image
Is undeserved
For these messengers around us.

emotions on a black canvas

The moon, pristine white,
Bore a hue of red today,
Looking at me intently,
Gleaming across that canvas,
So vast, so black,
Devoid her revering comrades
Who'd usually glint on that canvas
As specks of her grandeur.
She gathered ghostly clouds close
To render her emotions obscure.
Oh! Was it a blush so subtle
On that face so dainty?
Or a resentment
Heralding a ceaseless fury?

Slumber started to sail me away
In winds of epiphany—
Portrait of the moon hangs
Amid my thoughts aplenty,
For the artist is I, painting
Her emotions on a black canvas
Reflecting my mind's strokes—
Smudged and capricious.

akshay chougaonkar

One day in disdain, my reflection
Said to my shadow,
'You may be as real as I am.
Our existence surreal, yet mine closer
To his real life.'

The shadow agreed, lingering,
Still as light, replied,
'Yes, Comrade! His lifelike semblance
Exists in you, yet you are caged
Behind an open window, faux, perchance
As deceitful as you.'

Blank as a canvas, the shadow, now silent,
Persistent withal, said nothing.
Its accurate remark pricked
The contender in the mirror.
Soon, he walked away, fading the reflection.
The shadow dwelled in his company,
Perchance as a mark of victory.

A pensive moment stole his pondering.
Observing his own two conflicts,
He looked at two lights above—
Each glistening like fragments of life.
He yearned for darkness.
So, he turned the lights off,
Now embraced by moment of lull.

eclipse

Visible,
But this feeble display of grit
Is but an eclipsed
Mind that hides behind
A bubble of despair untold.

I hear a fable told
Of a glorified contentment—
Real as faux gold –
Like scintillating sliver
Around the sun invisible.

Listen! Oh! Comrade
Look around the moon –
Beyond your despair—
There lies true grit
That you must seek.

I plead you to end this eclipse
That binds your perception
Of this beautiful world
That exists.

Autumn Reminiscences

autumn memoir i

For many a wonted day
On my lonely couch I lay,
Perceiving these fall leaves
As autumn's final breaths.
Painting a masterpiece,
It smiles away to its death.

akshay chougaonkar

29

When on a frigid day,

The songbirds perched far away—

Their pinions fettered—

Sing an eulogy in an ardour faded

For autumn days,

A feeble smile escapes my face.

akshay chougaonkar

Scarlet crowns engulf

Ebbing green hues and enough

Conspires between the chills

And a winter nigh, but so still.

The crowns are a facade

For flames, leaving trees undraped.

those auburn trees

Lost in frozen time, I see
Through hazy window,
In the chills, the auburn trees
Vivid and exuding glee.

On a canvas of evening skies,
Under a sunset to behold,
Auburn autumn trees
Are crowned by the distant sun.

But as the sun sets,
I wonder—
Would those auburn trees
Be dethroned?

Every fleeting hue of sky commands,
In alliance with time,
Those auburn trees
Surrender their crown
And bow down to the night.

My unnerving gaze
Sees the crown fade
Yet those auburn trees
Merrily smile back at me.

Sly streetlights conspire with time
And thus, undaunted,
Those auburn trees reclaim
Their crown,
And proudly, I smile,
Hailing the autumn kings.

That misty morning
I saw golden sunrise caress
Dreamy blades of grass
Simmering nature's ceaseless hubris.
Chills thrived amid
A meek breeze of laze and bliss.

My sleepy eyes rejoiced
Seeing the weather on caffeine.
Dewy trees fluttered their grace pristine,
Like a peacock preens.
'Be gone!' At summer I had screamed,
My composure blown to smithereens.

Autumn's symphony was sung,
Another line in seasons crossed,
Resuscitating the poet
Bracing life's charade
And past's gambit that sought
Death of his words.

I offered the weather a toast—
A caffeine dose of my own.
My fickle mind found a heading,
And I picked up a pen.

the art unfolds

Each falling leaf
Is a brushstroke
Upon this land here
And the sky over yonder.

And I see a brush
Invisible
In this breeze,
Inconspicuous,
Painting autumn.
Distant hills watch
The art unfold,
Skies coax the clouds
To wear the same hue
As their grey
And gloomy dark blue.

Each leaf waltzes
To a unique symphony
Orchestrated
By the winds
And gentle rains.

I wonder
If it is a mural beckoning winter,
Or an epitaph of a season bygone.

akshay chougaonkar

Stories About
People and Places

wanderer

I am a wanderer,
Aimless withal
In life that is heedless
To the time that passes.

I run
Into caverns
Disguised
As safe lairs
For the night
On this hike
That is testing,
But seemingly
Innocuous.
The reality
Is more depraved
Than it seems—
A labyrinth
Hides inside
Murky cavern here.
So, I retreat
And stroll further
Into the woods,
Past wildflower meadows,
Under jubilant skies
That seem to recede
As I tread.

I am led
On a fathomless
Journey,
With nothing
But solitude
At helm.

A state of
Delirium
Makes me question
The reality
Of this solitude
That I yearn
And possess.
So priceless.

Then I wonder
If its coherence
Is merely
A camouflage
For a loneliness
That hides in my mind,
Lurking, waiting
To strike
At any sight
Of insecurity.

I move along
Unsure
Of what I feel.
These feelings
Change
With every shade
Of the sky.

I try
To side
With solitude,
But the landscape
Breathes air
Unfamiliar.
For now, I am
A wanderer
Lost.

the farm

This moss laden fence
Frames our little farm.
It is blessed by the sun
That kisses it ever so softly.
Oft times a drizzle
Sings songs of merriment.

The grass knows only of love
Falling in an embrace
Amid a graceful waltz
In a breeze,
Whilst it brings
Treasured music from farms afar.

akshay chougaonkar

I walk along, everyday
On these wee pathways
Smiling at the trees
As they gleam and wave at me
With a proud display of fruits
And I smile back in praise.

Cows and cats and pigs and a dog—
True hearted and friendly.
They surround me with their sounds
Orchestrating a symphony.
Ah! They spark a smile on my face
Watching them frolic the day away.

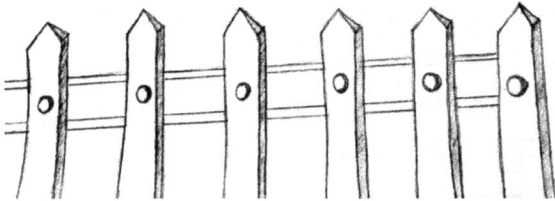

saxophone of the past

I am trapped
In a cyclone of notes—
This symphony,
Alluring, drawing me
Closer to a disarray
Of emotions of past,
Whilst these notes
Surround me, tightening
This noose here
Drowning me further
Into a reverie
Drenched in nostalgia.
I close my eyes:

I see
The same old man
From cherished memories
Playing saxophone
Under the old Oak tree
In the park so fond,
Where, in days of youth,
Knees were bruised
To sail paper boats
In cadenced streams
Born amid rains.

Singing songs
For the lost souls,
A distant Robin
Joins the old man.
Leaves sway in breeze
Gently, like lovers
To these notes.
Interlaced intimately
With a clatter of coins,
A crescendo play
And it passes
Like time.

Musician's hat stands proud
And taut, but tattered coat
Speaks of a grief,
Silently,
Amid a symphony
Ushered by brassy tones.
With much care, he plays each note –
Chromatic, bright,
Tremulous at times.
The tempo swings
And blends like moments
That forms one's life.

akshay chougaonkar

His music proffers
To people around —
A solace in these moments
They otherwise give up on.
These moments
In anguish, I try to salvage
And hold on to!
A child with a balloon
Dances to music.
He laughs and shrieks;
It belies his life
Of resentment and divide
Yet unheralded.
Hikers over yonder stray
From their path
Drawn to this music.

This symphony ends
And so does the reverie.
My eyes, teary,
Now see a lush ground.
It is barren now
Devoid the old tree
And the old man
With his saxophone
From the time bygone.
I walk away, slowly,
With an air of melancholy
Around me, building up
To conjure a new cyclone
Displacing
This cyclone of notes.

Standing tall, rugged and gritty,
He overlooked the horizon
Out of reach of sailors aplenty.
Hailed them with a haughty scorn.

Oft times he was draped in fog
Yet, he wore a pompous glow,
He defied winds that never stopped,
Flaunting his colossal brow.

River beneath raged at times
And often it flowed serene too;
He looked at her surrounding banks
And shaped her contours anew

But now he stands forsaken,
The birds his only friends.
No one hailed this bridge again.
Alone,
In his rust of egos.

the unloved notebook

At a distance, a woman scampers
From under one tree's canopy
To the next.
Not far from her a man dashes
And his red umbrella surrenders
Without much zest.

I see a toiling little stream flowing
Along the kerbside of this road much fond
In my memories.
Winds skim across its surface painting
It in autumn leaves—it is speckled in
Glistening bubbles.

Another man perhaps in his youth, hunches,
Sprinting with a purpose, clutching tight
His tattered notebook.
I look at the notebook in front of me –
Its flaking spine, barely holds together
A timeworn vinyl jacket.

akshay chougaonkar

My notebook is filled to the brim,
From the first page to the last, it is full
Of words like these.
Pages flipped across seasons, spanning
Eleven years, but today I realised
Not oft do I hold it dearly to my heart.

a lost soul

Sounds of distant brook allures her,
From this path rugged and overgrown.
Tempted, she looks over yonder
To find nothing but a vast land, barren.

Above, a Robin, perches in peace
In companionship of his trusted friend—
The towering pine, mighty and wise;
It is whistling with these chilly winds.

With dusk now approaching in haste,
She looks up at that wee bird jolly.
She pleads the bird to guide her soul lost
Amid this wilderness vast and gloomy.

The Robin heeds her earnest call,
And asks his friend, the pine tree tall
To swing its arms wide open
And embrace the lost wanderer.

akshay chougaonkar

Intimacy and Warmth:
Given and Denied

the path that she treads

The moss grows in the cracks
Along this pathway that I tread.
It watches all the feet that fall—
Some anxious and some upbeat.

But one day it saw an old man,
He walked slow past the lair of ferns
And in the next few moments short,
He dropped to knees so frail and rot.

The moss knew not why
The man fell to his knees,
But then his eyes swelled up with tears,
And red roses embraced the moss.
He thought of his beloved,
Laid to rest here beneath
This path that she used to tread.

another star in the sky

Tonight, there will be another star in the sky.

When the night
Embraces,
Faces fade,
And traces
Of those moments
Of pain
Saddle away,
With each ticking sound
Of this clock.

Pacified,
She rests in her bed tonight.
Through the window
That lone star sees
A fading twinkle
In her glazing eyes.
In her eyes, he seeks
A reflection faux,
Whilst those clouds
Slither in,
In with
Each violent gush
Of this wind here.

akshay chougaonkar

With each breath
Solitude soothes
Her mind further,
Hiding the ticking
Incessant.

In the night's embrace
Unfazed
By ghostly clouds
The lone star now smiles,
Oh! He smiles at her
As she gleams
Ever so graceful
Right next to him.

the dancing shoes

Dancing shoes look at her,
Their yearning evident
In the glint of their eyes.
Their black attire, elegant,
Puts on a lonesome shine.
This companionship
Stands futile.
A void subsists.

Pleading those slender feet
To soothe them,
The shoes desire their embrace,
A kiss that shall create
Something magical,
When amid a fervour
And tenderness
Their contours would merge.

She walks towards the shoes
Taking her time,
Envisioning a world surreal
That she would create
In this moment
Passionate and eternal.

A musician plays
Smooth brassy tones for her.
With much care, he plays each note –
Chromatic, bright,
Tremulous at times.
The tempo swings,
Slowly,
Leading her,
Outlining her body.

Time conspires with musical notes.
Each passing moment steals
Distance between the shoes and her.
A comforting sense of belonging
Ushers her senses –
Feeling
Each other's warmth now.
Her versed, bruised feet,
Now safe in the shoes' embrace.

Each note enthralls her,
Breathing life into dancing shoes.
She gives into gravity
For a fleeting moment,
Then contests –
Her foot skims through
Spirited air, blessed
By the old Oak tree.
Soon, there persists
A flawless synergy
Among her breath,
Heart beats, the moves,
The notes and the breeze.
She scripts a new story
Each time she dances.

The shoes, now alive,
For their beauty, they say,
Lies in her grace.

Tears welled up in her eyes
Streaming down along her nose
Like autumn leaves they fall
That cascade in wayward contours.

Trees here were draped in colours
But those over yonder shed so meekly.
A reverie drew upon her senses
As tears traced her cheeks so fondly
Like a caress from years bygone
That painted a smile, oh so dainty.
Like those trees, she had shed
And embrace that followed had set her free.

Her tears now rolled down further
Vanishing in subtle arch of her lips.
She was smiling, thinking of him
And so were those jolly autumn trees.

draped in purple

Who are you
Draped in purple and dainty?
Are you the one I know
Or do I see your soul masked?

Graceful, here I see you dressed
In a sweater entirely embroidered
In purple flowers.
But you change apparel,
Whimsical, like seasons.
In the days bygone,
You were amorous amid chills
And naked,
And under sunny skies
You fashioned a lavish
Green gown.

From afar,

In a merriment plagued by jealousy,

I see you dance a tango with the winds

That stride away apace;

Its caress unreal, deceitful –

Leaning in, leaving your senses bemused.

Every breath entwined with the wind

Your purple sheds unhurriedly.

Ah! The unassuming allure

Of the stranger I see here.

Who are you (now undraped)?

my dainty heart

What is it with my dainty heart?
It seeks refuge in other hearts.
Often, featherweight, away it blows
Like jolly dandelions in the breeze.
Other times, like a boulder, grief-laden
It stands motionless in time.

On this foggy winter morn
I sit alone with my coffee warm.
But then I realise, I'm not alone
When I see distant snow forlorn.
On it, the sun glistens in timid cheer.
I hear faint voices of my heart so clear.

I feel a gentle warmth in my heart,
Like hazy sunshine on the snow.
I have a candid talk, heart-to-heart,
With my heart that I for long ignored.
In a big embrace, I hold my heart,
And in togetherness, few tears we shed.

unrequited love

The clouds glide slowly across the skies
Heading to the sun kissed seas
And in their journey, they meet the mighty
Mountain, gentle and kind.

The mountain's crown has but faded—
The towering Pine trees bare.
Yet the clouds yearn to embrace
The mountain's mighty brow.

The mountain smiles at the clouds
Reflecting starkly in its lakes—
That is his heart, and in it dearly
He bears them all.

The clouds attempt to toil a descent
To live with the mountains wise
But the mountain drapes itself in winds
And sends the clouds adrift.

She looks at mountains, and sheds a tear
For, they remind her of him.
Sharing her heart drenched in feelings
The clouds drizzle.

ACT I: THE WOES OF THE LIGHTHOUSE

Rooted!

I am to this rock.

Daylight!

Ah! It casts me dead.

I hailed the sky,

It stole my spirit instead.

Behold!

My gallantry,

It is not fragile,

The populace believed me!

Unused,

It turned futile,

Too frail, they shunned me,

So, I challenged

The colossal sea.

Oh! Life and blithe, I beseech!

Why are you eluding me?

Horizon the hypnotizer –

It is ever changing and eternal,

Beholds me in its rapturous eye.

It stole my gaze

And imprisoned my mind.

A mystical maze,

Of time and tide

Entrances me.

An impasse; I fight

Until the fall of enchanting, endless night.

ACT II: THE TEARS OF THE MOON

My dazzle stands futile.

So spiritless,

Subsists the air around.

All in vain, I try to suppress

The brooding gloom and the oblivion

Prevailing all around

Incarcerating me,

Binding me.

I snivel.

These tears are invisible.

The stars mock at me, devouring,

Savaging my faith, now so feeble

A hazy gaze

Deep into this vile void,

And I yearn for the night.

A night devoid

The painful wait

And this longing sight.

ACT III: YOU SHALL DESCEND

Panoramic view

Canopied by skies

Painted in transcendental colours.

A lull lurks.

The scene turns purple.

From deep within,

From the horizon,

From the vastness of sky,

From the chasm of ocean

Shall free

Two solitary spirits –

Spirits of the moon and the lighthouse.

A joyous aura

Shall cease their wait, their fight

To be together.

The horizon shall be enlightened,

By their guiding light.

The day ends,

And the night transcends.

The moon gleams

And the lighthouse glows,

Oh! Glows his soul, deep within.

Thriving to unite,

They are the spirits.

ACT IV: YOU SHALL PART

The dawn slithers in,

A grief starts to bloom,

The glee withers off.

The spirits plunge into despair,

A sheer gloom.

They are in sight, so close,

Yet so far.

You shall now part

And return to where it all began.

Poems of the Fancy:
Little Joys Around Us

saturn's joy

Saturn swings from end to end.
He looks at comrades surrounding him.
Endless space and stars and void
Fills his life, yet not a voice
He could hear.

One day while on his routine walk,
He saw a glimmer wee
He glanced and saw these crystals stark.
Against a darkness he could see
Glistening rings.

He smiled at his comrades nigh
And to those far away he waved.
He showed them his rings of ice
Before they were lost or fade.

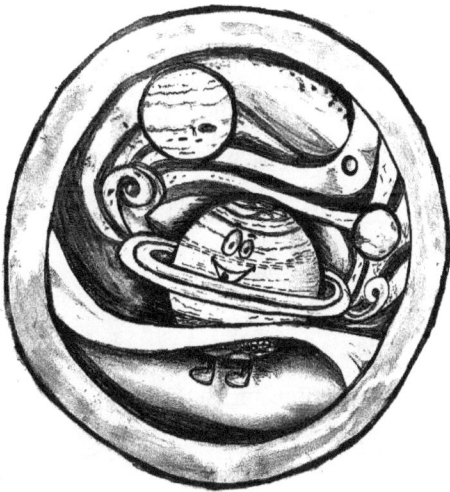

like the paper boat

Nuance of the youthful days,
Relics of your innocence.
Yearning, these wishful eyes
For candid rains,
At your depleted windows.

Times, when you made
That paper boat,
Like a world rising
In the mind of a poet.
Times, with a boat, you bent down,
Whilst the stream kissed
Your knees
And away the boat hurried.
A numinous mirth then
Adorned you face.

The boats are a past.
But they reside somewhere
At their destination last.
Epitomizing your bliss there.

Does the wind know
Where it goes?
Carrying unheard messages in tow
To people
Aimless as they roam.

Grass waves to it,
The lake dances
And splashes to its silent beat,
Cherishing the wind
Aimless as it roams.

Like a gritty messenger,
Across the valleys
It carries melodies and prophecies far,
Undaunted by hills,
Aimless as it roams.

Amid people and pets
In contoured alleys,
Being a part of their lives, an audience
To their musings
Aimless as it roams.

Does the wind know
My mind is quilted
In fallow thoughts?
It embraces me
As I roam aimlessly.

These foggy streets
I see,
Dreamy, after a drizzle.
These droplets on windows –
A unison they conjure
Streaming down, unsure
Of the direction.
But unhurriedly, they linger on
In the moment, on these panes
Then gliding down, creating an art form
Of their own.

High above, the fog descends
Onto these fields bustling with daisies.
My feet halt, and I sight nigh a bend
In a path overgrown with hollies.

Daisies are slowly consumed by time
Like spring by menacing chills.
Despite farewells bade, colours thrive
In autumn across meadows and hills.

So, I move on, embracing the fog that falls—
Listening to songbirds that sing year long,
Across seasons, preaching life to us all,
Smiling away merrily to their songs.

An epic fable is scripted
By the stars and the moon;
The sky they reign
As the endless canvas gleams.

This untold fable
Begins in the daylight,
Whilst they linger
Within a darkness,
Unseen,
Yet it always exists.

Conspiring with time,
And the stars aplenty,
The moon consumes the light
That hides the canvas.

Endless canvas
Presents an art surreal
With the stars and the moon
Reigning.

Time that allied with them
Now betrays,
Pleading dawn
To escape slumber
As this fable now awaits
Its denouement.

little flower

Little flower,
On these roads infinite
Beholds curiously
These wanderers adrift.

It blooms amid
These footprints left
On grass that looks
Ferociously windswept.

The flower delights
In their each step through,
Trembling in pleasure
From wee vibrations that ensue.

But, smiling at this familiar flower,
There is merely one lost wanderer,
For it is an illusion
Of a path trodden often.

Yon wanton trees are smiling
And chuckling and dancing in a frolic,
On their own, gracefully swaying;
And oft times with the breeze –
Embraced by an invisible lover.

I wonder if the rain elevates
Senses of the trees to a happiness
We once knew but lost.
Or perhaps, the rain drops
On their way, through the sky,
On to the leaves, trickling down,
Merely tickle them to a playful joy.

have you ever

Have you ever stood atop
Distant hills or covert groves?
There in the untarnished air
Surreal sound of silence lingers.
Glorious silence deafens there
The sweetest songs that birds doth bear.

Have you ever touched the trees,
Felt their bark 'neath your fingertips—
Felt the same breeze on your skin—
And the sunlight that blankets them?
For it is a joy so sincere,
Not many moments of life doth bear.

Have you ever realised
Scent of a dewy winter morn?
Reminiscent of campfire
Extinguished to the glowing embers.
A blissful scent in the air
Not the fondest flowers doth bear.

akshay chougaonkar

Epilogue:
The Stories Behind This
Book You Hold

Fallen leaves crunched under my feet
As notes of distant miners brimmed.
Cutting through stone, I imagined them,
Under warmth of a nascent sun.

I walked past a lady draped in black,
Grieving over a pile of stones.
Her farm perchance stood there once;
There now lies buried mere bones.

An old man in his coat scruffy
Hailed me in his spirited walk.
His saxophone bowed at me
And played for me a silent note.

A muffled murmur of yon kids
Speaks of a candid innocence.
Their sole toil is chasing butterflies
Frolicking on those grassy fields.

They know not of wanderers adrift
Or about a broken dainty heart,
Or of one autumn lover who tried
Painfully to keep her lone star alive.

The kids then relinquish their frolic
When the faint symphony starts –
Notes from under the mighty Oak
And from above it, the songs of birds.

A solitary path, covert so far
Emerges, crafted by travellers
All ambling towards the music.
But I seek the songbird in the Oak.

At a distance, forlorn bridge stands
And from atop it, Ravens
Watch earnestly over creatures.
Weeping moon in bridge's arches
Awaits nightfall, whilst a Robin chirps
Guiding songs in nearby pine groves.

I wiped a tear, and then some more,
Flipping pages drenched in poems.
Then I cherished a smile that grew
When I saw that songbird perched
Atop those branches bare anew;
Its notes imprinted in careful words
In this book that you now hold.

Thank you for reading this book.
It would mean the world to me if you share your thoughts as a review on any platform of your choice. You can also share your thoughts on perceivingthings@gmail.com or @perceivingthings on Instagram.

www.ingramcontent.com/pod-product-compliance
Lightning Source LLC
Chambersburg PA
CBHW032151020426
42334CB00016B/1265